# SUPPLEMENTARY STUDIES
## for Flute
### (or Piccolo)

R. M. ENDRESEN

## PREFACE

The **SUPPLEMENTARY STUDIES** are designed to supplement or to follow any elementary method. The important features may be summed up as follows:

1. They are musical.

2. They stress not only the technical side of flute performance but contain many fine cantabile passages for the developement of tone quality and phrasing.

3. Excellent material for review work, and reading experience for more advanced pupils.

4. Their construction is conducive to accuracy, the rapid passages being intersperced with easy passages. Therefore, useful as preliminary to the perpetual motion type of study so much in evidence, in the advanced flute study repertoire.

5. The length of the studies prohibit boredom, a very important point in teaching young players.

*R. M. Endresen.*

*B. Mus.*

# SUPPLEMENTARY STUDIES
## for Flute
To be used with, or to follow any method

## 1

R. M. ENDRESEN

## 2

# 3

**Moderate Waltz time**

*Fine.*

*D.C. al Fine.*

# 4

3

# 5

# 6

# 7

# 8

5

# 9

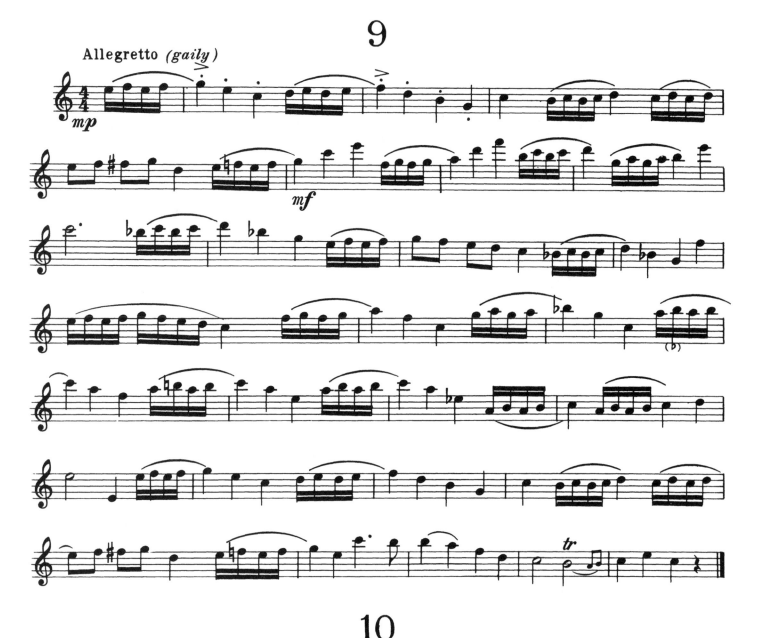

# 10

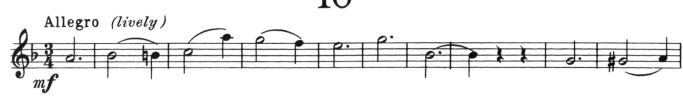

# 11

# 12

# 13

# 14

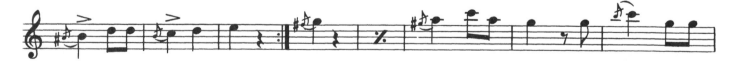

# 15

# 16

Practise slowly – gradually increase to rapid tempo

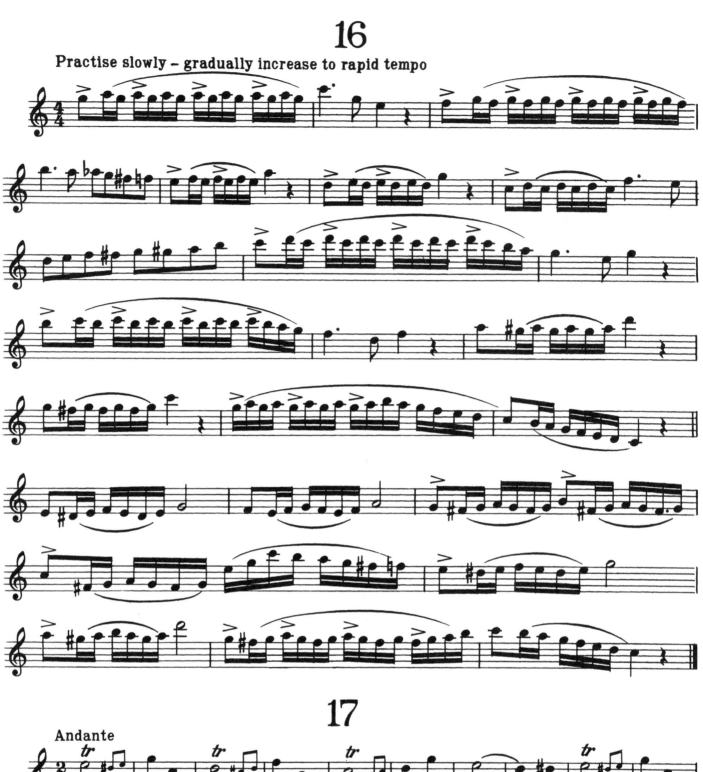

# 17

Andante

# 18

Tempo di Valse *(fairly quick)*

# 19

Marziali

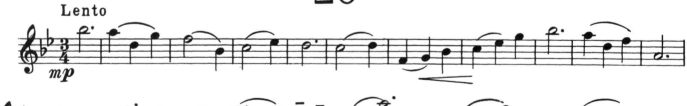

# 20

Lento

# 21

**Moderato Espressivo**

# 22

**Allegretto**

*rit.*  *a tempo*

# 23

**Moderato**

*mf*

# 24

# 26

# 27

# 28

# 29

# 30

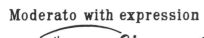

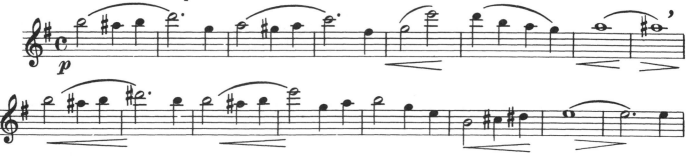

No. 30 continued

Animated

# 31

Staccato

# 32

Andante sostenuto

# 33

Theme moderato

**Variation**

# 34

**Grazioso**

# 35

In strict rhythm

# 36

Marcato

22

## 37

Andante cantabile

# 38

# 39